T0380629

JOURNEY TO THE OTHER SIDE OF FEAR

AMALIA VANMATRE

BALBOA.PRESS

A DIVISION OF HAY HOUSE

Balboa Press books may be ordered through booksellers or by contacting:

Balboa Press
A Division of Hay House
1663 Liberty Drive
Bloomington, IN 47403
Www.balboapress.com
844-682-1282

Print information available on the last page.

ISBN: 979-8-7652-5238-3 (sc)
ISBN: 979-8-7652-5237-6 (e)

Library of Congress Control Number: 2024909863

Balboa Press rev. date: 07/12/2024

Contents

AIR

EARTH

FIRE

WATER

AIR

Twos and Sevens

Dreams never sleep
All… just a thought away
In the lack of limits
And presence of opportunities
Dream freely…
Say it and sky will understand
What will come is epic
A series of completely random
Carefully planned coincidences
Tokens of magic
Crystals of hope
Independent of anyone
Directed by you
Guided by the stars
Propelled by inspiration
No one can piss on your flame anymore
Nothing can destroy the real…
Take away, control, change… you
Signs and hints
Amulets of future memories

The Other Side of Fear

Hello pain… hi again
Come on in… sit! why don't you stay a while
I'm listening… so let's talk
Won't run away or hide this time
Gripping terror… overtaking
In a stronghold… squeezing tight
Panic-ridden… choking… paralyzing…

You don't scare me anymore
Not just because it can't hurt any worse
Because now I know there is light on the other side
And, I can't wait to get in front of it.
Yes, it's late…
Soon, it will be too late.
I so look forward to that glorious day!

Waking up from an illusion
Malarkey of your world
From nowhere to now here
From dis-ease to peace
From alone to all one
Closing all old wounds…
Calling back my power

Through this painful rebirth
You created a superhero
Teaching me…
Redirecting energy to change
Nurturing self-love
Finding peace in grounding
In this new chapter of light

Solo Act

Life is a solo act…
And youth escapes so fast
Like a box of matches
We slowly burn out

When pulled out from the scheme…
Simply an anti-definition of reality
And it all could just be in our heads
Life… this process of dying
Turns out to be intriguing
There must be a purpose… to wait

You're all alone
As you dream your life
In your little perfect mode
Creating the best you can imagine

We come alone, live alone, leave alone

Questionnaire

Is it worth it… dreaming and the effort?
Isn't it all our imagination anyway?
If so, why don't we envision any better?
Apparently, we like the torture…
Masochistic nature of the troubled minds

Ultimately… do we ever get what we wanted?
If masters of our own creation… why don't we rule any better?
Could it be impossible to even dream in a perfect mode?
And if that's just our own invention…
Should it not prevail in our minds at least?

It's got to be the law of equilibrium…
Fool is the one who believes they can decipher
… Complex character of the basic instinct.
… Naturally, very unnatural to some

Twice

First is not a test
First is a lesson
First means naive
First is vulnerable and unclear
First… you think you know…

… Until you learn

Second is not a mistake
Second is familiar
Second means experienced
Second is prepared and strong
Second… you know…

… But do you?

A Mile

What seems possible at a time
Is so inevitable in retrospect
Brevity, gravity, serendipity
Become unscared, untethered…
Collect only tokens of time…
Memories of love, connection, warmth

Untrue by an inch…
Untrue by a mile

Irresistible

Desperately friendless or in need of a hand
They give so little… and expect so much

Self-contained or independent
Opposites are wedded in the end

Damage proof or love-resistant
Non-verbal cues reveal much more

Analyzing the intentions… to the core
Tempting victims… still unconsciously

Doomed for failure from the start
… Drawing lines around irresistible

A need to belong can lead so astray
Like a string tightening on a reel

Tempted to search through the unknown
So far from nature… away from home

Before experiencing more
She already knows she's lost them all

Human Beast Friend

Slipping through the dark
Speeding extension of a human body
Tamed beast of the future
The one to trust…
… They become one
Protected from all things outside
Where peace turns into madness
And silence screams so unbearably
In alchemy of sounds… roaring voices of the wind
They're alone on the road
In this overwhelming tunnel of darkness
Peacefully cradled in a friendly bullet of steel
Imagining time travel through space
There's still so much to explore
Maybe the sun will rise tomorrow
… No need to make amends

Fallacy

On a quest for knowledge
The fruit of truth… the end of lies
Justice of the sustenance
… For the curious eye to find

Grievance of the fallen…
… Through the hazy centuries.
Don't you want to know it all?
It's been done for you…

… Consume and don't question.
Enclose… enfold… pass on…
On a mission, bound to be saved
… Those in costumes are the pranksters

Confess… renew… pretend…
Preying on your ignorance.
What is obvious… not yet acknowledged
Brainwashed tools

In the hands of the righteous order
Oblivious to the greatest power:
The gift of choice.
And why is he a man?

Multiselves

All descend from way beyond
Tumbling down into crowds
Aren't we all mixtures?
Aren't we all spotted?

Jeopardy of imaginary superiority
Breeds in prideful minds of fools
So, why exactly are you better?
What gives you the right to judge?

The more power they have
The more cruel they get
In all corners of their minds?
Ignorance in trade for violence?

With the curtains of curiosity drawn
Behind the walls they've created
Why do they so incessantly hide?
Is the maze of meaning so unyielding?

All of this… not new to us
It's all in their heads of steal
Secrets of the human thought mythology?
When exactly do they know what they know?

Billions of years again…
In between them and themselves
Don't we choose what to believe in?
And what if there's just us?

Wake Up

Human nature… deviated parasitic culture
Preying on life… claiming to protect it
Assumed domination for precarious reasons
Documenting evolution of the self-destructive monsters
Complicating its existence…
Or just trying to make it look better?
They don't come here to just hang out with you

Irreverence is ever persistent
Arrogantly…
Less in touch with themselves than ever possible
On the outskirts of society
The deeper we dive, the closer we get to the end…
To the truth of it all
The essence of existence

Humankind just became endangered species
Sometimes…
What you don't want to believe in
Is the hard cold truth
Staring you straight in the eye
Sensitivity…
      Essentially…
           Results in self combustion
I know you wanted good…
So far from truth

Ironically, the truth is the end
… The transition

For Sale

From their mouths
To our ears
Digest it all
Find the sense
        What is real... you can't figure out
        What is an illusion... we black out

Everyday, our minds like landfills
Overflown with trash forever

They say
We accept
Tripped up
We lose our stance
        Why do we conform... do we know the price?
        Sentencing "unique" to die... is all we are a sell-out?

Everyday, our thoughts recycled
Foreign property... we're redesigned

Everyday we feed on garbage
Like a sponge immersed in poison

Everyday we degrade
Each day...more of us for sale

Vulnerable volunteers
So willingly sacrifice our freedom

See the Sense

Buried on the sun…
Living in a trap…
Hollow people…
Collective… senseless life…

Grab your luck…
To lose it soon…
Earth's got sick…
Malfunctioning fools

… Moon's your friend…
Watching over you every night…
And she won't give it away…
Cause you live to dream…

You still have to choose…
In an endless fight…
Save yourself…
Or save your life…

You'll never understand…
People of the clouds…
Vs. people of the flames…
Never together… yet so close

EARTH

Blue Planet

Friendly home or a deadly trap?
Mother earth or the first to die?
Liquid heart of warmth or a nuclear time bomb?

We dig and push, do all we can
It's a madman's chase to precarious destination
Illogical selection of the trickiest ones

Western man, business man, simple man… betting to determine the end
While she's getting knocked out by own parasite in an all-time match:
"Blue Planet" the Earth vs. "Ferocious Predator" the Human Kind

Would we stop striving had we known the end was near?
Or can a human outlive the earth…
Becoming a malignant tumor of this solar system

Stone Grey

Rolling overhead
Swallowing… covering it all
Silver blue
Hanging heavy
Unfazed and calm
Very much alive
In a rhythmic breath
Wave after wave
A warm shroud
Of comfort
A familiar place
With a kiss of light
At the end

Earthly Existence

Layers, and layers, and layers…
As if in an onion dress
The more you uncover, dig, and peel
The closer to the core of it all
The essence, the knowledge,
The matter, the spirit
Layers of beauty, textures, smells, and colors
Layers of warmth, emotions, touches, and feelings
The meaning of this earthly existence

Leafing

Clearly... all the leaves must fall
As multi-colored butterflies
Release, fly free
Accepting, as attentive passengers
Independent, yet knowing their roots
From united to fragmented
The lessons are plentiful
Pain-free... liberating
Beautiful journey... when in present tense
Turning yesterdays to memories...
Tomorrows to inspiring thoughts
Embrace and let go of the moments past
For that's what they are... gone
Painting all in warm tones of comfort
Lead not follow
Trust the fall
Jump into the abyss
To find you... perfectly whole

Christmas Tree

Hail…
Christmas tree
Don't even try to be mad
It doesn't matter… just die

Decorated corpse… for all to see
Paradoxical sign of birth dying here… all alone…
Before the admiring eyes of ignorant spectators
To please them…

Ornamented icon
Surrounded by smiles that don't see any deeper
And there's no one to weep for you
Just as you become a memory…
If you do at all…

Dead metaphor of all that's fresh and new
Victim of desire for natural beauty
Hijacked "home" so far from home
To bring happiness to the ever-killing beast

Sorry I can't save you
Just as I can't save myself

Faux Leopard Fur Coat

They hide among us
Or… are trapped here for a reason
Those who see more… the angels
The liminals… the troubled minds
The tools… all them apples.

Their world so much more vivid
Provides a broader scope
Scintillas of magic hidden from our eyes
Their efforts to color our lives…
Go so unnoticed.

Rants, snarls, grimaces, monologues…
Not pointless or misplaced
Aimed to teach us, show us… open…
Depths, dimensions, and flavors
Of realities we choose to ignore

They're meant to challenge
The inherent limitations of our small minds
The little tea pots, visionaries, and fairies
Frantically doing their best to catch our attention
While we insist on healing them
Or, at best…
Forcing them into a label

The United States of Hope

Universal security failure…?
In company of unnatural hate… on religious grounds
In a matter of one hour…
Suicidal mission… in the name of god
The model of political righteousness…
To run down the prosperous nation of "democracy"!
No frustration… hit them back!
Vengeance in the name of freedom…
Armageddon of trust… global mushroom of loss.
In debris of humanity… the need for support… hugs… assurance…
That there's still time to strike back… get even… kill them
Disheartening World War III…
The last chapter of hope…
No future for the desired coexistence.
Why aren't we astonished by the extent of moral damage…?
The inevitable end… right behind our door
It is where you too will crash…
With the collapsing world's unity
Orchestrated end of the world… by own human hand.

Good Morning City

End of an era? ... politician's stroke
... And... the Oscar goes to...
Man badly burnt in a home fire
Tomorrow, few snow flurries, 32 degrees
Miners are missing!
Man kills his wife, daughter, and her boyfriend
Accident near ridge rd., disabled truck on main rd.
Families experience anguish...
Weekend will be warmer and sunny
Mother... cut, beaten, and bound with duct tape
Miners survived!!!
New school opens, police patrol the traffic
Cats and dogs for adoption - visit local SPCA
Boy falls out the window
Group of American soldiers killed in Iraq
Miners are dead...
Seems as though they watched each others' backs though
Little girl found dead in a house fire
Accident south bound lanes
SPCA opens at 10:00 am awaiting adoptions
A lot cooler today... some snow activity
Traffic slow south bound and east on lateral
Crooks steal a statue of Jesus... thieves!!!
Wall of bricks falls on firefighters
Violence flares up in Iraq
Miners are dead.
Find out why your electricity bill will go up... at 8:00
For more pressing news, visit: www.city.com

F for Fake

Miss you…
And your fingers around mine.
But i can never forget
We can never be innocent again
You destroyed **us**… and you did
Murderous monster… slithering snake
Tomorrow has been canceled
You'd been dismissed.

Haze, mist, fog, Spanish moss
Off road tracks…
All the mystical trails…
Desolate wilderness and woods
Fire roads and lighthouses…
Lakes, evergreens, crisp mountain creeks…
Evaporated, expired… too far gone
… Not coming back… not ever… not the same.

Distant memories… lingering on
Purpose…
To cherish or torture?

Habitual Corporate Absurdity

Welcome to the phase of gainful growth
The dimension where evil free-roams

The space of lies
The weight of hate
The lakes of quicksand

The world of dog eat dog and obnoxious backstabbery
With a strong dose of pervasive condescension and belittling

The core of illness
The river of disease
The source of uneasiness

Chiefs, and boards, and the whole executive mess
Abusing so casually, anything but super simple

The realm of fear
The world of anxiety
The source of stress

Overtaking ugliness of constant intimidation
Illusionists' trap with deceptive vision
Not a milk and honey land
More of a dead-end… a nowhere way

Conartist

Why does he never intersect?
As if he didn't want to participate
… But he never did…
So if now is different…
Why not now?
And if not now, then when?

What is holding him back?
From living the moment together
Connecting, exchanging points of view
Learning, growing, seeing, touching…
To feel alive… for the first time in years
Ironic… as it seems

Guilt and shame of betrayal
Shrouded in his gravely secrecy
More wounds… much deeper than our normal road rash
And he still shares the body with the man from last night
But he should never be allowed to…
Carry anyone's heart in his hands again

What if she was a healing tea he drank?
Helping him… draining her…
He now needs to find his own way in the darkness

To-be, Who-be, Lost Bee

Possessions, impressions, admirations.
Time is money…
So they say
Sacrifice your true self
To impress others today
Big house, fast cars, rich friends, lap dogs…
A yacht!
Make-believe life fulfilled
Can't afford to look inside?
Or are you unequipped to see in the dark?
Many stop signs.
No-outlet paths…
Where you are.
Isn't it a waste how you lost yourself
Where the money rules.
Life confused…
You are… Bill who?

Macabre Tale of Real

The worst of crimes is soul abuse
Somehow the body heals and forgets
Scars fade and no longer startle
But the soul bears the hurt.
Stabbed, neglected, abandoned…
Having been bruised forever
Carrying the weight… and profound sadness
Planted by someone else's hands
Is a tortured soul

Replace questions with answers
Problems with solutions
They say…
This can provide some consolation
So i reach deep inside…
Only to find pain and sorrow,
So much sorrow…
So much it's crippling most of the time
And the echoing, haunting scream: "why?!?!"

This world doesn't seem to know
How to take the edge off
Or provide a good old "make it all go away"
Soul bandaid
Or the answer:
If you take enough wrong turns,
Do you end up where you would have if you took the right one from the start?
What is it then:
Forever more or nevermore?

FIRE

Tequila and Lime

High fiving one day
And lynching ruthlessly the next
So hard to see this as a favor
Hope? or a noose around my neck…
Persisting… leading me on
Only to throw daggers and darts
As I race straight for them

Binds… thick and heavy
Wrapped so tightly around my heart
Sinking it to the bottom.
Crashing once again…
Yet another fall
Fighting to come up for air
Strange how I bend but have not yet broken

So tempted to stop
Just let go… let the blade come down
Notice though… how so far
It's not been enough.
Unexplained forward push…
With no option to pause…
As there's still more to climb.

Fighting back the bitter tears
Trading in for a nice, forced smile
Fake…? or hopeful…? or a fool…?
So simple and so impossible just the same
Hurt beyond what I think I can take
Stumbling into dark of the past
Where joy is so heavily dappled with pain

Some of those memories torture me still
How can I forget you for good
When you reappear like that
While I thought I've just healed…
Why did you say you rescued me
But then you fed me to the lions?

When will the bad be just enough more than the good?

Untamed

You don't need to understand anything about me
And it's not for you to know me in this world
Whether or not my darkness revealed itself to you
We did the soul dance just this once

But now I'm a secret
You don't have the privileged to discover
Or hold, or brag about, or share.
And I like it like that.

You can't read me… try, do all you can
I'm an enigma, beyond what your mind comprehends
Put labels on me, capture me in your words
And we both are certain that you know you're wrong

I cannot be owned, or known, or tamed at all
And all you got was a single swirl in flesh
That's enough to awaken so much in me too
Cannot take anymore because I miss you so

Subterfuge

A whole half of the equation
Inner rant… inerrant
Self-perpetuated
Primitive mind
Impetuous… disharmonic
Dissecting your thoughts
Chameleon illusionist
Indelible like your own shadow
Unscrupulous monster

"There is no wrong or right
You are wrong and I am right"

But

Half and half equals whole
Whole and whole equals infinity
Just as your lie lasts a moment
And truth lasts eternity

Stabbed a Million Times

The sun rises every morning…
With such arrogant disregard
For the earthly beings
Everyday…
Leaving no time to despair…
To grieve, to cry, to feel everything so deeply.
Till it sets… vanishes
As if it never was
Relentlessly drowning yesterday's carnage in the dark
Returning yet again to illuminate persisting scars
… The stamps of time
Forever reminding of the horrid pain
Their wounds once inflicted.
A chance to die enhances growth
Instilling the lessons chosen.
Dying 36,000 times
The cycle repeats until release
A cruel human trap machine.
Days… an illusion of time
That simply never is…
As the spirit grows
It can never be broken
Although it can be abused…
But can it ever be lost and then found?

Alchemist

Riddle me this…
Maddening feedback loop from hell.
If you never struggled you never lived?
The alchemy of life… soul of the universe
Think in reverse
Impossible is possible.
Unpack your past… don't look back
Burn it all… with intention
No judgements, no assumptions
And the whole non-fuckery.
See what's in front of me
Divorce the child, the mind-fuck
The oppressor, the abuser
The parasite, the leach
Turn problems into solutions
And all shit into gold.

Stuck on You... No More

Every step leads astray
When mind and heart don't see eye to eye
Actions rape intent when words are betrayed

You were just a sequitur
Nothing more… than a kidney stone… a turning point
Defining ambition neutered by self-doubt

      Motif… spot it…

We don't make mistakes… they make us
The time is finally now
And I'm the wild card…

      The missing link…

Helping you see both realms
Grounded… spread out like tripod's fingers
Reflecting nothing but the truth

Aware of this kind of superpower
You have been canceled
And you won't fill my eyes full of tears again

And by the way… in a way…
Not all questions have been answered
But everything is an answer

Coalescence

Nigh an evanescent memory
Still so close
But almost beyond reach
His energy, so unmistakable…

She still remembers his silhouette
His blurry face then painted with sadness
They're still in the room
Together, but already apart

Her hand on his chest
His eyes already staring beyond hers
But this is a temporary goodbye…
Though neither of them know that yet

She's guided by invisible hands
For once she knows she can let go
Love, joy, pain, or sorrow
They come as they must

All she can say now…
Is:
See you… sweet D
On the other side of night…

Why You

Boiling up…
Spewing…
Flooding…
Fighting to come out
Overcoming everything
Clouding the mundane

I'm choking on the love inside
Enclosed… waiting… ready
Storyboarding what is to come
Piece by piece
Image by image
My reality unfolds

Don't know where my heart belongs
But it's clear it wants to be by your side
While your loving arms enfold me
I want to see
I want to see it
I want to see it all!

Leaping flames
Glowing embers
Crystals of hope
Sprinkles of magic
All of me misses all of you
All of me wants all of you

Pick me up
Pull me close
Hold me tight
Lock me into your gaze
Dare enough to stare into my soul
Let's run off and experience it all

Soul friend
Connected by light
Bringing the color in
Discovering what joy is made of
Side by side…
I have a feeling I'll leave my heart there

Soon

Don't yet know who you are…
Here in this world
Yet, I miss you so profoundly
Don't know what you look like
But I'm certain I will recognize you.
Don't know how much time has passed
But I'm psyched to reunite soon
With your genuine stubbly smile
And your charismatic sunny aura
Blondishly magnetizing me…
Shifting my focus…
Changing my direction
Making me think about
How much I just want to…
  Dive into your eyes
     Sink into your chest
        Melt into your body
           Disappear in your arms
Protecting arms that hold me tight
Skin on skin
Hand in hand
Soul to soul
Equal parts
How's it possible
To miss a life I've not lived…?

No Trespassing

Only you can swim in the silky sea
I don't let others dive in
Some tried to soak their feet...
Not easy when the sharks await

Storms get wild when you're gone
Defense mechanism it seems...
Protective nature of the quicksilver waves
Or maybe you have cast a spell... ?

V vs. H

Like a neuron... all or nothing
The way we are
Equations, calculations, computations
Perfectly dispersed...
Led by perceptual set... see what we expect
Senses united... we produce the world
Important... often left out by occlusions
Like in motion parallax...
Changing views as we turn
Determined by preexisting knowledge
Like the lines that converge as they become more distant
Paradox of mind against us
All humans... all alike
For good and forever
Atoms, molecules, chromosomes...
In attentive inattention
Eyes belong to others
We adapt the perceptual organs...
To benefit at our own expense
Visual images... not an explanation
... Far-sight, near-sight, cross-sight, fore-sight...
As in aerial perspective - farther is less clear...
The way we are
Your perspective, my perspective...
Sometimes intersecting
Skewed reception

That Night You Stole Me for a Dinner Plan

The doors swung open with a graceful force
… A grand entrance without even knowing it was
Locking eyes in our very first hello
And a pinch of animalistic sizing each other up

Like pianists about to deliver most powerful concertos
We sat down across from each other
Not aware yet…
That this was the beginning of our little masterpiece

A heartfelt embrace brought "us" into life
You were real in front of me… and ever so consuming
In split seconds, minutes bled into hours
There was no stopping after this green light

Craving you was my biggest weakness
All my old tricks faded into oblivion
No crutches to help me out of this
So I immersed myself in all the passion and love

Instantly graduating centuries in just a day
No more infatuation, games, just sex…
Leveling up sharpens one's standards so fast
Not ever hungry for less than all that

WATER

All Encompassing Energy

Neck to neck
Level-headed and balanced
Transcending centuries and, in fact, all time
Friction-free, magnetic and pure
Equal wholes, manifesting

Can't go back cause now I know
Those lessons are now complete
Progressing, cheering along the way
Illuminating the truth
The answer is the constant

It is clear…
No need to believe cause now I feel
Radiating all-encompassing energy
Consolidating…
      Integrating…
          Mostly…
               Not hesitating

Los Otros

The lucky star ones… unite
Opportunity is on your side
This time, it's all the same… to find the other different ones
To bond and to thrive

Find the missing parts…
The 'between me and myself'
Collect souls to grow
Unpolluted, un-conformed.

There is something hidden out there
That only they can see
But who is who, and how to see beneath the camouflage?
Aren't we all meant to be alike and looking?
Are we even aware…?
Or are we just wasting away…
Baffled souls… having to come back again
As one of these others who crave to seek and know.

One Divided by None

There's something sleeping in me
Something i know only you can wake
Signs of…
Culmination of my tension…
What's the intent?
Spit it out already

Too anxious to even tremble
In meridian of my madness
Some place transient and unclear
Solemn captive of my mind
Refusing to wait any longer
Just feel free to change

Recovering from a swarm of thoughts
Once again, they try to divert me
This was not where i belonged
But the road is getting clearer now…
Benefits of hindsight
Follow your heart, not your mind?

Collaboration, relation, elation
Correcting the offbeat perception

Ocean

Ocean of thoughts rolls murmuring by my feet
Can't stop the waves from licking me...
Set out to devour my existence
Furious lead-blue sky, dropping overhead
Merging perfectly with the quicksilver sea
Feels like I'm free… out here

Flaws stick to us like scars… not around here, no they don't
Each time I float away from the mundane
On the waters of timeless days
Along the currents I navigate
Unable to see the shore
Feels like only home… out here

The waves crash gently now
Reaching me with their softest touch
They're the only ones who dare to speak
While all these eyes out there take all I have…
So I'm hiding from the looks that steal.
Feels like I'm safe… out here

Ampersand

Don't know where "I" start
And where "I" end…
Anymore
Maybe "I" go on forever,
Or maybe "I" am just a blip

Everything started late…
For me.
Everything…
So delayed I may run out of time
Even time to catch up

Falling behind or just not my time?
Refuse to want to expire.
Curator of my own story…
I am my own spice, my own inspiration
And I've got the backstage pass

High Tide

It's got to be true - they can't just simply invade…
But I'm not sure I quite believe that.
In essence, in a sense, "me" is all we have…
Is it not right to protect it?

We get lost when we hand our power over
Sometimes it seems we're just like glass
Permeable to the eyes waiting to peek in and plunder
Would a disguise do?

How to get back to the place
Where words don't bounce right off the walls?
And I wonder… have I completely sold-out
Or am I just better at fooling you?

Isn't it bad enough that we're already sharing our lungs?
Only now I become invisible…
Something went terribly wrong…
I'm not mine anymore

… Sleep forever, dream forever
Dissolve, diffuse, disappear…

Torn

With a heavy heart…
I barely choked up a tearful goodbye
To your…

Painted sides
Strong mind
Love when looking in your beautiful eyes

Funny side
Wet sloppy kisses on my face
The neck grooms you offered so scarcely

Field-fresh breath
Kind soul
And head tucked underneath my arm

Sensitive nature
Confident stance
Persistent tail swish, as if I was a fly

All the gentle hugs
The outward silliness
And ability to completely melt my heart

Inquisitive being
Playful character
And clever pranks you so enjoyed

Non-negotiable stubbornness
Unbiased fairness
And the black and white, always so perfectly placed

'Hello' knickers
The silky coat
And your hooves' sound on the barn floor

Patience for my mistakes
Focused look when I called your name
And all the mud you brought in on your back

Occasional 'I'm not so sure' snorts
With the pounding heart
And wind and hay smell in your mane

Curiously perked-up ears
Colorful personality
And your withers with impeccable views

Ominous presence
Way of showing me you held a grudge
The crunch of a carrot in your mouth

Lush black & white tail
Cutest smiles and goofy faces
The irreplaceable feeling when on your back…

Miss you already and always…
And love you forever
My precious friend
My Sol

Drifter

As if against the grain
Struggle to connect
Word wizard is now so quiet
Has the well gone dry?

Talk to me!
Highly combustible…
Hyper sensitive…
Excessive in everything… where are you?

Aberrant need to spit it out
Stellar carcass transitioning
Renegotiating and transforming
Nothing can wrong or intimidate me… anymore

Can't steal my experience
As I assemble myself
Generate, ignite, and inspire
Turns out the well moved abroad just for a while

Tranquila

Light as a feather
Letting go of the pent-up
Release the disease
Turning skin inside out
Remove distractions
Pouring heart into intent

     Grounded but free
     High yet wise
     Fast but calm
     Limitless yet connected
     Grateful but confident
     Respectful yet unconstrained

In unifying views…
Create opportunities
Following what feeds your soul
Trust the love within
Slaying the worn archetypes
Emerging unscathed

     Allowing the universe to fill you,
     Circumstance to propel success.
     Cultivating self-respect,
     Recognize and know it's you.
     Believe your path,
     And water yourself with love.

Being still… be quiet
Listen, breathe, and feel
Connect to your true self
Un-constrict your reality
Mastering relations to all
Where no one can impact the core

Red

Life is but a game of dice
Equity only a dream
Days run out of time
There has to be a purpose to die…

> The blood is spilled now
> More reason to poison than rescue

Now her hands… old and empty
Grief welcomes everything she is
Resignation is a noose she's weaved
She can't rest until she leaves…

> The blood's been shed now
> More reason to poison than rescue

Back then… everything withered, once and for all
Ever since… everything's painted in his blood
Her life now useless… she suffers alone
… Her bitter thoughts wallow in all red

> Now, the blood's been spilled
> More reason to poison than rescue

Weakened, she opens to pain
In volatile perception of what's fair
Decimated life of the only one
All her dreams, forever stained in red

> The blood's been shed now
> More reason to poison than rescue

Whenever she wakes, she bleeds all over
Her wounds ripped open again and again
Vexing questions remain unanswered
Why did he leave? why? why is she still here?

>	He's blood's been spilled now
>	More reason to poison than rescue

She knows...
She will never see him smile or hear him call her mom again

D-dill

The goddess is distant
She is naked and shy
Her body draped only in snakes
She had been raped... you know...

Snakes' eyes protect her
She hides by the temple
Out in the sun she lies
Tropical aura is so soothing

Exotic goddess
She's absent and silent
The goddess' been stripped
She had been raped... you know...

Her soul engraved with meaning
Her tears... bitter and heavy
She has been hurt, she has been wronged
She had been raped... you see...

Die Unsatisfied

Sun sets
No time… no time
To wait
You better run
Don't look back

If you misuse your time
Abandon your mind
You'll have to die
Unsatisfied

Set your true north
With eyes wide open
Shooting for the stars
And, fly…
Fly high

When in the end
There will be no amends
You'll have to die
Unsatisfied

Get up
Leave behind
What doesn't serve
Create a temple
Of unconfined one

And if you fuck up this time
There will be no going back
You'll have to die
Unsatisfied

When you lose your shape
You become else's shadow
You'll have to die… unsatisfied

Printed in the United States
by Baker & Taylor Publisher Services